AFTERBURNER

Peter Porter arrived in Britain
lived here ever since. Since
native Australia often and consi
present-day poetical worlds of b
he has been a freelance literary journalist and reviewer.
He has published sixteen books of poems, plus four
further volumes with the Australian painter, Arthur
Boyd. He has been married twice and has, with his
second wife, nine grandchildren.

Also by Peter Porter in Picador

Max is Missing

AFTERBURNER
PETER PORTER

PICADOR

CONTENTS

ACKNOWLEDGEMENTS

Thanks are due to the editors and compilers of the following magazines, newspapers, periodicals and anthologies in which some of these poems appeared: *The Age, Ambit, Australian Book Review, The Best Australian Poets, 2003, Eureka Street, Harvard Review, Island, Moving Worlds, Orbis, Poetry Ireland, Poetry Chicago, Poetry Ireland Review, Poetry Review, The Shop, Spectator, Times Literary Supplement, Vintage, Water Rat Anthology, World Wide Writing.*

AFTERBURNER

The Last Wave Before the Breakwater

The engine dies. The dream has by degree
Come to where the green is lightening, the rocks
Are somewhere in the civil distance – sea
Is moving up in mist, a paradox
Within this calm. Something is now to be.

The storm is distant, just the lights behind
The eyes are left of lightning's ambuscade,
But still the swell is present in the mind
And now the panoply of waves is made
By memory and allegory combined.

And it is here, the last surviving wave
Which starting years away was following,
A true occasion which the heart might save
Its courage for. A very little thing,
It says to die, to rhyme into a grave.

And know the dreaming self will not relent
Or convalescent mind afford its hope,
The voyage ending here before its end,
No harbour lights, no casting of a rope,
Wordless, auxiliary and irredent.

Mi Diverto

And if the world be mad
And tied up to success
With hope of trading good for bad
Dispersed as 'more means less' –

And generations strive
To push their children on
So one blood line of all might thrive
In one dominion,

And this be plain to each
Since History sat down
To plan anew on hill or beach
A truer sort of town,

Then why contrive an art
Touching not the least
A juster, fairer, kinder start
Or sure place at the feast,

And fashion at the desk
Instead thought's sounds and shapes
To make what consequence at best
Will buy in books and tapes

Unless it is to please
The oldest animal,
A self of brain and jointed knees,
The bored obsessional.

Mouth

In the deepest parts of ocean
fish have mouths larger than
the remainder of their bodies.

As if a Brooklyn God
told them, 'You're all mouth,'
and they quipped, 'Just like you.'

They look ferocious
with self-lights and goggle eyes
and acid-needled teeth.

But might they just be,
courtesy of depth and difficulty,
unable to disguise themselves?

How big then are their sphincters?
This same God has sacraments equally
of voiding and consuming.

He's fixed mouths as bottom notes
of a chain of harmony
all the way to silence.

In our little surface world
he tells us how to swallow Him
via a Eucharistic fissure.

Killing a Mosquito

I slap the mozzie on my hand,
the blood is mine, the black its all,
a million years of contraband
that this one second might befall;
it can't, but I can understand
the rule – in whose court is the ball?

What said of it that I should kill it
since late or soon I'd have to scratch?
No password, sesame or millet,
urged: *lift the multi-treasured latch.*
As well defrost a piece of fillet
and brave a blood this blood to match.

When Francis Bacon wrote that men
fear death as children fear to go
into the dark, he dipped his pen
in blood as light as ink; he'd show
the fretful soul that what might happen
was quaint as killing a mosquito.

Why Did Dante Pick on Suicides?

Life is someone's gift. Dante thought it God's.
Doggerel or great verse or what's to hand
Can warm the afterlife. The *Afterwards*
Of Hardy trades full stop for ampersand.

And this is not great verse. It's written for
Those loved unhappy shades whom Dante turned
To sticks and marl. Forget the every Law
Of Trespass: peace may be strangely earned.

Holding On

We were embracing, as always in dreams,
unexpectedly. There was that warm
and wide-field sway, part arousal
and part the oldest visitation
of good fortune. How would it change?
I wondered. She I knew was dead, but
my portentousness was proof I was alive.
Amid the planetary uprush I was sure
I would not have noticed the dividing
line between the living and the dead,
radiant here in her beneficence.
And then the words of Pascal intervened.
'We break each other naturally. The evil root
of men is hidden, not pulled up.'
We knew, love, we knew, and we held on.

Deuterothanatos

I have found a poem in your childish hand
carefully dated, 'aged thirteen years, ten months',
which speaks of 'the low golden light'
and of the coming of what, unknown to you
as such, is surely death. Though we are born
once only, we die several times. If our
single entitled death defines us, something
of it may be shown beforehand. In
the poem you greet the unknown greater world
with a sweet bold welcoming sign, almost
an entreaty. But what confidence remains
that on that lonely morning when you died
your seeming change proved true, and that those calm
confiding words had not been overwhelmed
by terror? I see myself revealed
in solemn Greek proceeding hand-in-hand
with airborne Hermes, second-
guessing what's to come – with you ahead,
the light already low, and perhaps goldening.

The Rider Haggard Window,
St Mary's, Ditchingham

Time which eats the stories of our lives
Preserves a cruel freshness here to show
How energetic certainty contrives
To tell us what we think we almost know:
The warlike God of England will bestow
At least in retrospect on loyal wives
A school apotheosis, dirge of knives,
With dying, quick in life, in glass made slow.

A dubious transfer this, as history cools,
An ancient trespass, but a change of rules.
The world was opening which today is closed,
And where the mind went, destiny would tread
With God and Science noisily opposed
And story-telling garlanding the dead.

Lares et Penates

For Christine

I dream that my enemies like me
And animals come to my hand.
I question my three-tiered entitlers,
There's so much I don't understand.

These silent yet sibylline whisperers,
So spotted and cat-like and calm,
Give blessing through painted-on whiskers
And keep desk and writer from harm.

My dreams come, they murmur politely,
From bestiaries quite of my own,
And Nature's an hermaphrodite
And Man is God's feminine clone.

Away from my desk's apparatus,
Asleep in a turbulent bed,
I leave the warm shore of a partner
To wander the land of the dead.

O save me, Penates and Lares,
My porcelain mute Trinity!
Remind me if idle or ardent
Who here is my best enemy.

The Second Law of Clumsiness

There is a compensation for Unbeauty –
Not ugliness, a spectrum-end of power,
But mild equations of the Not Quite Right.

Start banging about, feet turning in and out,
Challenge the Epigone his Master's name,
Unreel in taffeta a change of scene.

Not you Hermione! When truth is weighed
It feels like lead. The Primary Law will let
The farmer prise the piglet from the sow.

But, ah, the Second Law. We drove all night
And stumbled into Paradise. The Virgin
Chose not to see the Juggler miss his catch.

Progress has Depression printed through it
Right down to the last indulgent suck.
Why spoil your perfect mien with candyfloss?

Work backwards from Macaulay, meet the clumsy
Clever child. Is anything more naff
Than *Walking with Philosophers* on the box?

We're working on The Third Law. It may have
To do with Economics. Or with Love.
Or whom the Promised Land was promised to.

Sleeping with the Alphabet

You glorious twenty-six, not equal
In purport, short straws of words,
Come with me in the night-time squall,
My hurricane of verbs.

My chiefest pegs to hang fear on –
Don't think it's only sights
Which dreams call up – Wordsong
Lingers in the tucks and sweats.

Sounds of pre-performance, cries
Subsumed in nothingness,
Hoping to syllabicize
Themselves as messages?

The A of Anger, E of Death,
An I who might not be myself
And O the deadly wind that bloweth
Unto U, my vowel of Truth.

Mutiny of the Bountiful

The plum survives its poems.
WALLACE STEVENS

How would you know perfection is a hurdle
Not of itself, but in your art of praise
Having changed your mind on Raphael several times?

A richness in right places, saturation,
And nothing extemporized or dandified,
Almost a closing down of disappointment.

Time – which has chaired this maturation,
Itself uneasy – tells the categorical
That even the pungent clove has relatives,

The auto-ritratto is a kind of lie,
The clouds on Eden were for colour's sake . . .
And who looked up to clap the claim of rain?

And almost like the surgeon's fine incision
A beautiful face emerges on the screen
Slicing itself away from averages.

What should the spectrum say if Gulliver
Or some such realist quizzes it for worth?
Which number-cruncher watches from the sand?

Convene an epitaph for epigraphs,
Pronounce that plums are primary compulsion
And poems full and hieroglyphic fruit.

But write at shorter length. In plainer style.
If Stevens's furore 'choreographs',
Your flummery should be content to dance.

And notice how your terror floods the cup
After a night of wrestling with the moon,
That inner floss behind the door of death.

It does you credit to be calm. You're learning
To want only a piece of magnanimity,
A sliver shaven from the silverside.

The garden changes colour by the hour.
Yet does it? Is it the world in words suspended
Which eyelines edges of the bountiful?

The Man Who Spoke in Tongues

He found he couldn't find his hand
once here today was gone demain.

His train ran fast, his train ran slow,
but he got off at Subito.

Those Pentecostal flowers he bloomed
were multi-cultured in one room.

His watch sat silent on the table –
time was another Eurofable.

On isles where parts of speech were pigs
he truffled up some infra digs.

Having to leave the colloquy
he made his anthropology.

His every course had as its par
the contents of the minibar.

When Lawrence-like they buggered him,
he cried aloud in acronym.

And knew, with no word of a lie,
a thousand ways to say Goodbye.

Sex and the Over-Seventies

You thought it wouldn't worry you again
but comes this Second Adolescence,
the never-mastered stripping of the Bren.

And now the bodies cease to rhyme –
disappointments not relieved by joking,
dignity grown hirsute by the hour.

The curse of Literature – MacNeice's Horace's
Lycidas, who makes young men a furnace,
is only a midnight memory of Boarding School.

Hope to be someone's 'Ancient Person of My Heart'
or even a 'Maimed Debauchee' –
better than Herr Aschenbach on beach patrol.

And cringe when fellow-males anatomize
delusions of their female friends
with vernal blood-flow from sarcoma sacs.

It's late and you and your body
are alone – keep talking, to delay
having to go upstairs together.

Masculine Endings

The death of everything, we say, must be
Ensanguined by each single death: once strewn,
The blood applauds in magic resonance
That stringing-out of time we codify
As evolution. Unhappily, we try
To round off every action, and keep accounts
Mortality will underwrite. In poems,
As in life, we set out to avoid
The extra syllable, a child in mother's arms,
Stressing, for male completeness, the end of line.

Komikaze

Each of us thinks he is a suicide
(and we do too, the women say), and this
despite our fear of disappearing
and losing the discipline of self-distrust.

And Comedy will make it even better –
Saint-Simon's bowels exploding at the Court
and showering shit on ermined sorrowers,
with Heaven laughing at true reverence.

You need to judge the moment to go mad.
Nietzsche heard a tortured horse's scream
and recognized his cue; but Turin now
is just an average sound-frame of complaint.

I'm sure my Father lived so long, not out
of fear of death, but more because he knew
he hadn't the profile of the Great and Good
yet wasn't needed where the damned are stowed.

The old joke goes that we sophisticates
will be surprised by hideous prods and pains
from hornèd devils just because we think
such torments silly: already we've seen worse.

Is death a joke? Depends on who is laughing.
I have a friend who tossed into a grave
an Avant-garde Review to give the corpse
some reading matter for eternity.

Lingerings of the Cheshire Cat

Turner's pubic studies still troubling Ruskin's heart.
That second-best bed of type, Anne Hathaway's Sure Start.
Tell them in Lacedaemon we forgot to bring our cameras.
Fish preached at by St Antony, forever after stammerers.
A saint's eye or a drunkard's eye rates Yeats another Whig.
'Du bist wie eine Blume – Ja!' Beauty is a pig.

Harriet Wilson's cool advice – publish and be dined.
Sherman to his Band Master, 'It's Georgia on my mind.'
Marvell lost to Poetry, fronting *Affairs of State*.
His bladder, not Lord Rochester, stoking the debate.
What should they know of Kipling who only England know.
The quothing of Poe's Raven and the boding of Hughes' Crow.

George Eliot to head again the Check List of Chick Lit.
Yes, there's honey still for tea, and death to go with it.
At Rilke's Testimonial all angels on the pitch.
'Elle est sourde, mais elle paie' – Igor Fyodorovitch.
A billion years, a billion stars, just one to Bethelehem.
They knew not God or whooping cough, and so we gave them
    them.

Ideological Moments

The history of emancipation.
Overtaken, riding uphill.

—

To wither away the state must grow a tumour.
This lesson is from Capitalism.

—

Infinity is Nothingness reversed.
Nothingness is Infinity continued.

—

Wittgenstein thought wealth a defilement.
Another disappointed inheritor.

—

Capitalism, claims Kolakowski,
is a perfect fit for Human Nature
while Socialism is Impatience's ideal.
Thus selfishness shall make us free
and magnanimity enslave us.

—

Arts Administrators,
more numerous than Artists.
Labour Legislators,
more timid than the Chartists.

Born on the Left
he had to think well of his fellow men.
Born on the Right
he tried to think well of his enemies.

Those who believe in something
and those who believe in nothing
say they despise the credulous
who will believe in anything.

The way to Hell is paved with good inventions.
Misprints are Truth's non-contributory pensions.

Classical Poetry didn't rhyme
although, of course, its language did.

The choice before today's Sublime
is adding to or getting rid.

———

I saw him looking lonely,
The big man in a blazer,
Reading *Il Gazzetino*
In the Sala di Attesa.

Now, where's the ideology
In writing things like this?
John Berger would know how to
Reveal what is amiss.

A rentier will be framed by
His clothes, his seat, his habits.
Gainsborough would paint this one
Pot-shotting only rabbits.

———

Pascal spoke in Mathematics
    Of Reason and of Love.
He warmed his hard theology
    At Descartes' glowing stove,
Knowing he could never rhyme
    Down Here with Up Above.

Clear Air Turbulence

'That sparrow-flight, my mind!'
ALBÉRIC OF TOURS

'Chips of ill chance are fallen amid my choice,
To mar the mind that meant for to rejoice.'
GEORGE GASCOIGNE

How long can an evasion last? Whose mind's
In flight? The poet's? Why invent a monk
Who never was to hint that learning is behind
Dubiety? Is doubt, like history, bunk?
Too many questions loom – let verse behave
And freely associate with turbulence
As if the sentient air-bag of the grave
Might at the crash perfect the present tense.

And so it happens – on a placid day
Among the flowers of circumstance, a boy
In boring heat is struck down on the way,
(Kicking against the pricks, a broken toy),
And stands beside the flapping canvas boom
Which insulates the bare veranda, screams
He's seen the face of something in the room
Which is the sheen of death, which in his dreams
Will ever after be the world he knows.

Heroic men of one-time felt the same
And dared a war of twenty, thirty throws,
Saw torture smooth the field of blame
While gross believing centuries kept out
The ordinariness which fillets compromise.
A cannon creasing stomachs was the snout
Of Lucifer; repentance stained the skies.

The unmade creature, out of boyhood's grasp,
Might never guess the hour of its end
Or that small time could wear the endless mask
Of history; but be ready to rejoice
In this scanned ordinariness which wakes
Upon the pillow and listens to the voice
Of average expectancy and makes
Some dilute resolutions for the day –
Command and sex and amity and charm,
The ease of choice, the freedom of delay,
Impossibility of serious harm.

The flight whose destination no one knows
Will follow the Great Circle of the earth,
That tactile aether where the death wind blows
And is not felt through portholes – booked at birth,
The coward spirit questions why the sky,
So clear and so prophetic, still suprises
As what's invisible dilates the eye,

Convects the blood where the horizon rises
Or dipping wing incises as a blade
Through nothing – pure implausibility
Has put this night-time creature in a raid
On life – he may be vectored on the sea
Or pinned by gravity to his seat,
But everything his mind makes has a clause
Whose one instruction is repeat, repeat –
Staying aloft both breaks and makes the laws:
The drink in his hand spills on his neighbour's suit
(Apologies the self will understand),
Such turbulence is common on this route.
His is a flight that's destined not to land.

Why Are We Waiting?

Suddenly the God of Repetition clears
the air of early afternoon of boredom.
I'm watching our resuscitated goldfish
on unsleeping infinitely repetitive
patrol in their nice new light blue
scientifically oxygenated tank.
They don't know this is perfection,
that their propulsive purposelessness
is not, as I have sometimes taken it to be,
a theatre of despair, like nightly dreams
encompassing living while we sleep,
but rather an involuntary dance
adding symmetry to necessity.

Perhaps it's not perfection, but defeat.
Yet how could these unthinking creatures
ever conceive of anything they might
be conscious of as an intentional goal?
As one self-serving watcher who can see
nothing which is not a paradigm
of his trapped nature, I have let my eyes
be drawn to a world of limits utterly
stifling in its lack of will. Perhaps then
I should suppose, as one more compulsive swimmer,
I must trust to boredom, not to reason,
to steer me safely through the glass confines.

Loony Loach Is Dead

Why must you die?
Last week you were frisking
round the tank, playing second fiddle
to the goldfish.

Soon you were unmoving
on the carpet. How could
you know it wasn't the stream
promised by your body?

Thinking of yourself, says
the fantail. Yes, but I want
to thank our little loach
for this morbidity.

The way is cleared, the road
to death is empty.
The truth is, loony loach,
we are all going nowhere.

Well, Francis, Where's the Sun?

They buried him in this complete basilica
But let him roast the Umbrian countryside,
Brother Sun, baking hard as silica,
With Clare, as clear as conscience, by his side.

But where's the sun today? Its canticle
Is sung by orphans on a pilgrimage.
The sun's not in his high conventicle
As Maga bends to wash the feet of Mage.

Brother Wolf and Brother Body, pity
Brother Sky's minute particulars
Which must conceal in serendipity
The love that moves the sun and the other stars.

The Deed's Creature

The President, the Pontiff, the kick-arse CEO,
Have playground massacres to come to terms with.
Books have told them conscience will bestow
Only an affidavit on their myth.

They are centaur-making and show us why
The melding must be monstrous if the end
Should rate a fresco – that she will have to lie
With De Flores is Beatrice-Joanna's overspend

To seed a modern creature. All of us
Are actors of our uncompleted natures
And though a god or some conspirator
May strike the better profile, once the fuss
Is through, we watch, amid holistic chatter,
Culture conveyencing the Minotaur.

Horace's Odes Translated

The fine scribes of America are herded here together,
The subsidized Aediles, the Ivy League Grammarians,
    compilers of historically flattering parallels,
    beneficiaries of a Military-Industrial Estate –

all are between the covers of a well-printed book
to honour the lightly louche Italic poet who
    loved both boys and girls and knew best how to please
    the hard men of his time while nudging memories

of Nature on remote selections and showing how
Republican directness could mutate to slaves' long service
    (a dab hand at rebuking lusts of gilded youth
    while hinting at the use a girl might put her bangles to),

but always and ever the querulous protester at
fate and extinction, whether wandering after Philippi
    or narrowly missed by an old and rotten tree,
    reborn among the countrymen of Bly and Cage.

Throughout this book the Classically-conscious reader
can scarcely avoid the shadow of a new Imperium
    falling on the old: after all, the Parthians inhabited
    what is now Iraq, and it upset the Emperor

when one of his pet legions was brought home
in body bags – nor do the parellels stop there
    since the English Augustans still haunt the stacks
    and every university seeks a personal Maecenas.

Was it all so unimaginably different and all so long ago?
What stays the same is place-making, pleasing the Sub-Dean,
    keeping language Pastoral while hinting sex and booze
    may, after all, be just another way of working out.

Eheu fugaces – we learn to sigh and greet a Postumus
in every generation with comradely decorum –
    America may pass away, and Europe, but will singers
    of tomorrow's *carmina* reflect their world so well?

Rimbaud's Ostrich

He didn't need one, he was an animal,
The animal which outmanoeuvred Europe.
But in the photograph, as on a boot-polish lid,
The ostrich struts cross-legged, a mapping stool.
Harar is four thousand miles from Paris.
And just a Metro ride from two World Wars.

We should ask the ostrich what it thinks
Of scholarship, or lurid nights with absinthe,
Of being in the months of love for essay prizes,
The coal-smoke-crystalled walls of Camden Town,
The semi-educated painters jetting in
To put some Prester John in Cork Street daubs.

France deserved this tribal fetishism,
Its language had become mere logarithm,
Its classicism a blunt guillotine.
Supposing Rimbaud met Sir Richard Burton,
They would have ridden ostriches round town
To startle the solared anthropologists.

Rimbaud at Charleville

You were loitering, friend; I got a call
from the *Saxon Barrow*, our only decent pub,
'There's a potential troublemaker come to town.'

I speak through my magic time-tube, since I'm dead.
My palely florid French is good Australian.
For punishment they've sent me back to Charleville.

This is it, friend. Not such a hick joint as you think.
Half my friends are Public School boys; I get cards
postmarked Venice. This is a proper country town.

I came to the boil too soon. Why didn't I simmer
as a Second Empire Poet? Some drunk asked me
in your Marble Bar, 'You a Calathumpian Dago, Mate?'

That'd be Basil. He's been rude ever since he discovered
he had a pansy name. There's a big guy writes in the papers
says three-quarters of our land is set aside for mystic poetry.

I gave it away at nineteen – even Jesus kept it up
till he was thirty-three. Under the railway arches
in some Grand Place I foreswore Europe's heart.

I don't go a bundle on this Multiculturalism
but hospitality's something else. You can be Français
or anything, but just keep telling us we're tops.

I said, there's the Carpet Moon, *Théodore de Banville*
at The Oyster Bar; *there's blood slopped at Sedan*
and The Being Beauteous Album, 'le bruit neufs'.

Everyone's got a home town. I was sent away to school
with a thousand dollars in my pocket from kangaroos
I'd skinned. Uncles Eric and Neville never came back from France.

Where is your Bibliothèque Nationale? I asked, and they
directed me to the School of Arts. The Emperor
is with his 'spectacled Accomplice' and his smoke.

It's a privilege to have a Great French Poet here
in Western Queensland, but as my old Headmaster used to say,
'Thank you for coming, and when will you be leaving?'

The blond soil, the nevergreen, the eucalyptus frosting
in my eyes – What's happened to the Ardennes? I'm
playing chess with Ras Makonen in a louvred SleepOut.

The Jesus ewes are lambing and we round them up
on Harley-Davidsons. It's a working day, Mr Rimbaud,
don't you go frightening the drinkers and the parrots.

Applause, Oblivion, Tumours, Absolution!
The je *I called* un autre, *the democratic feet*
beneath the table! Jusqu'à *Charleville, I'm dancing.*

Isaiah's Knee

(St Agostino's Church, Rome)

That knee alone is worth the price –
Michelangelo told Raphael's patron.
The other knee is covered by voluminous
gold drapery. What he holds
for us to see is blazed in Hebrew
while framed behind him words
are carved in Greek. But sight's
a Pentecost and bad-tempered seers
may pun their eager way to Heaven.

The Guide Book states this church
was where Top Girls chose to pray
and meet their learnèd clientele.
Rome is Resurrection, not
Renaissance. They kiss the foot
of Sansovino's butch Madonna
to bring love home – myself, I'd choose
to touch Isaiah's rugby knee
and hope the courtesans were generous.

Outside the church what's left
of the Campus Martius dazzles
in the sun. They told me as a boy
that Catholics left the Prophets
to the Protestants – but here's Isaiah

firming up the old Republic
and guarding what was once a pagan
titulus. He stares ahead, stylite,
promising another age of masculinity.

In a Time of the Wilting of Poinsettias

That Christmas is a secular feast
Few could deny or likely wish
Were otherwise, and so at least
    It will be thought outlandish

That presents round the plumpish tree
Swelling the profits of the Bourse
And profaning the Nativity
    Should seem par-for-the-course

Of ignorant consumerism –
Go draw a better gentler line,
Say through a giving gesture's prism
    The light of love might shine –

See stacked up on the carpet's pile
Appropriate or unwanted things
(*You're worth it, you're an audiophile*)
    As Christmas Morning brings

New Magi to suburban lords,
With carols from King's College or
Bach's camels at the Jordan's fords,
    Sit-Coms and Shows galore

To mark the presence of a God
Not gone away, just lower wattage,
The Casa Santa where He trod
　　Transported to Swiss Cottage.

And now the strangest gifts are strewn
Beside the electronic Crib
Unseasonal poinsettias soon
　　Gone like Sennacherib

In briefest scarlet metaphor,
Poor tropic-loving petals forced
To feign eternal Summer for
　　A cold doctrinal North.

But theirs will be an apogee
Indifferent to the handset's search,
Not showering leaves round the TV
　　But properly in church.

Look almost anywhere in Rome:
Ablaze in ranks of white and red,
Poinsettias blooming far from home!
　　Christ's living spirit fled

From Time to Cross and Altar and
Ciborium – the white His semen,
The red the suture of His hand,
   Duality His demon.

A mobile in a tourist's coat
Reorders the Canonic Hours.
Inexorably downward float
   The spent incarnate flowers.

Ocean Beach, Sorrento

(Painting by John Perceval)

(For Peter Steele)

Mr Perceval has left the washing up
    to dab the canvas; detergent foam
has frothed inside his eye, a hiccup
    of insightfulness. 'Out of loam,'
says God, 'I've fashioned a creature who'll find no home.'

Mr Perceval, hearing the call, has come
    to where the sea is sorting out its drinks;
it means to go home pissed. Rocky rum
    and gin perturbed by sundry pinks.
God again: 'A difficult world for an animal which thinks.'

Mr Perceval uses tempera and enamel,
    God's not a painter but he scans
both sky and poetry; he can spell
    Heaven, if that's still in his plans.
He presumes, 'The proper study of Mankind is Man's.'

Hearing Chimes in Carlton

From soul to soul
        miniatures of Heaven
                or the lifeblood's swinging bell
On the grass the soulless doves
        so taciturn and slight
                only striped by time –
And this to be a list
        of Last Things winged to first
                some workings of the sun.
We moved to the celestial
        caught by the ordinary
                the half translucent things –
It was poverty and fear
        then opulence and doubt
                scripted only by old age.
Every Magister appeared
        in dreams and gave instructions –
                follow your ferocities
You hearing what love is
        self turned inside out
                the hard skin of the heart
A truculent innocence –
        what you did to hurt
                your parents and your friends

Was set to music in
                those paid-for other dreams
                                those sketching opuses
Of sounds, alternative
                universe of doubt
                                of forgiveness never known.
And chime-bells hanging
                in a sunny atrium
                                are a call to war
Attrition for however
                long it takes to reach
                                a reconciliation with
What can't be reconciled.
                These chimes we know are what
                                exists in abstract thought
When Mind admits defeat:
                'things' and 'places' will
                                nest in the lymphs and glands
Only the course of blood
                its sad reticulation
                                sentinels our ears.
Someone from a seminar
                is going to say these lines
                                are mere Parnassian
Words trying to ape the harmony
                of dissonance and assonance –
                                please make them something more!
A quiet turbulence
                telling us that all strikes
                                are firsts and lasts of summoning.

The Jews in the Ice

After Abraham Sutzkever's *Farfroiene yidn*

Then: have you seen what death's mad vision yields:
The Jews, row on row, in the snow-covered fields.

They lie down quite breathless, cold marble and blue,
Yet death is not in them, for death freezes too.

And somewhere each spirit shines on in its grave,
Like a fish with its golden fin flecked in a wave.

They do not speak, do not whisper, but stay sunk in thought –
The sun in the snow is too chilled to report.

Each frozen lip's redness burns on in a smile,
No movement can welcome, no word reconcile.

Close by its mother, a young child lies curled;
How can she suckle it, in her finished world?

That uplifted fist of a naked old man.
Such power in a gesture, such weight in a span!

Till now I have tasted all deaths that there are
And none has surprised me, the near or the far.

But here in a street in the heat of July
The cold pricks my skin like a lunatic's eye.

And once more towards me the blue bones advance –
The Jews in the snow-covered fields look askance.

Oblivious marble is coating my skin.
All words come to nothing, no light can get in.

Each movement is frozen, I'm like that old man
Who lost in the ice raised his powerless hand.

Le Promenoir de Dorothea Tanning

I am old now and find the world just like
an album of the works of any one
of fifty distinguished avant-garders shut
away in drawers, politely gathering dust.
Art is necessary, we all said, necessary,
not imperative – if we'd been proud
of what we did with the intensity
of personal vanity, our art would have had
no value. That's the wonder of it, that's why,
daring the outrage of offended orthodoxy,
we played excess, contempt for ordinariness,
gross showing off, a love of money
and celebrity, a purging of
highmindedness – we left enlightenment
to Art Historians, showed on canvas
or set in metal the outside of the self.
Surrealism, some said. Reality, we claimed.

In barren lushness natural to Provence,
among the warriors of *boules*, we raised
one of our totems of New Mexico
and christened it our Volto Santo, vending
the vapours of old age, piping entrance to
an Underworld of European pain.
I walk here now that Max is dead; I've tamed
the poetic landscape with the Devil's word,
Set social knowingness down among

the Nature Worship of Cézanne, who might
as well have worked with rulers and a compass
to fix the terrible mathematics of
his vision. Colours should be characters
in a comedy, the linear mesh so loved
of Florentine perspectivists be stage
directions, changing Paradiso with
some witty sleight-of-hand to Luna Park.

In Chicago we would say, 'Render unto Art
the things that are Art's and unto Chicago
the things that are Chicago's.' And such things
they were, since blood on stockyards never dried,
since Tammanies and brute Philistia
set up the only new coordinates
for Art in modern times. The Whitmanesque
which everybody loved was newness folded
into oldness, with all the colours of
the ego glinting. Our old was new, Pound's bits
of culture which he wrongly mourned dressed
as charming scarecrows, the funny side of death.
I go walking with my soul now, closer
than dog or angel or stopwatch,
a painter shunned by paintings, airing a self
unalterable as a photograph.

Thank God I still have Seillans in the dark,
this feverish gloaming where we roamed, two souls
already somewhat elder when we came.
You thought that you loved Paris, but I knew
how German, almost Grünewaldian
you were – and I was self-confusing too,
thinking my personality more fine
than slaughterhouse America could hold.
When was it that we learned the truth about
this fabled France, that it is just a filter
for the genius of other lands, its Classicism
Le Grand Monarque or Emperor on the make,
not Europe and its louche imagination
but custodianship and old presumption?
France stopped dead with taxidermist David
and left behind for its inheritors
a necropolis to play mortician in.

We were cartographers of Kitsch and made
of it a Pantheon of Purity
which purer spirits commonly betray,
yet still we spoke of casuistries
as old as Acheron. Our dressing-up
was to revive those incidental mouths
of prophecy named Sibylline – a joke
that Michelangelo devised butch ladies –
Cumaea, Erythraea, Delphica –

to gloom along with God and heavyweight
Old Testament depressives: he prayed
to be no artist but to run a farm
a little way from Florence, and this our house
is our modest *podere* from which
to look on nothingness. Our ghosts may walk
along the ruined aqueduct to Fréjus,
pro consular and lecturing the dead.

And on the Beach Undid His Corded Bales

Who was it led us to overestimate the New?

The Greatest Living Poet's recent volumes
are in a stack at your left hand – what do you do
in between getting on with your journalism?
Go back to his earlier and more sprightly days
when his difficulty was felt like sunlight
cool along your face, when you decided,
notwithstanding your resistance, as you claimed,
to literary fashion, that this intransigent
dandy got the world into his impure verses
as almost no responsible rival did –
so much so indeed that a jaunty episode
among the Check-Out Sylphs, an Ode to a Torpedo,
or some sort of squirrel-hounded sexual outing
in the Allegheny Mountains seemed, as you read it,
a calm reflection worthy of Matthew Arnold
minus his Rugby gloom and moral nimbus.

Welcome to the Vale of Indirectness.

I think I am like Schubert's 'unglückliche Atlas'
carrying the world's weight on my shoulders,
which might be glossed as resenting my banker neighbour
walking heavily across the floor above my head,
not for the noise he makes but because he's
a reminder of the glare of truth which first
intruded on my childish sight – there is no money in poetry

but there's great poetry in money – ask Robert Browning.
My neighbour dresses for the City in decent grey
with perhaps a dash of scarlet in socks and tie,
and at weekends is seen in jeans and sneakers,
unlike Matthew Arnold, whose Victorian raiment
flares only in the gorgeous blood-wrap
of his death wish. How could he
and Clough have been such friends? Easy, says
the melancholy of dark days, they shared a cosmos
of despair; the one sought some relief in loss of faith,
the other in not ever having known it.
And they have a colleague in the syntax
of their language. That's where you must go
if you would find the secret of Victorian Art,
a Mad Hatter's plethora of logic
and dementia, a railway-carriage molestation,
their works bogus Gothic, Miltonics for back streets,
facades not just for Tennyson but Sex-
Tourism. To please the death-god in their sewers
they transported hope beyond the harbour mouth
to meet with dengue on the Irrawaddy or murder
on the gold fields. What we have today
is a collage of the various inappropriatenesses,
an inventory of style which knows
so little about living and far too much
about excitement. Then, at least, let the latest
of us make utilitarian and cluttered screens

to hide the fact that no one's here. Arnold's shy metaphors
are growing tendrils: when we find ourselves
on beaches we should offer up a prayer
to a seriousness engraved like coffin lids.

A Strange Resolution

The Emperor pardoned Gombert for his buggery
Of a choirboy – it should have meant the galleys,
But Art must seek in sex crime or in thuggery
The Morning Songs of Satan and his allies.

'They're playing our tune,' said Mary when she heard
One of the eight Magnificats of Gombert.
So sound may suck the marrow from a word –
Give or take a rhyme, that's quite a tombeau!

The stars sleep soundly in their numbered dorms.
As veterans of cosmic song-and-dance,
Their preference is to hear chromatic storms
Resolve in eternity on a consonance.

With Blinds Pulled Down

Mozart auf der Reise nach Prag

We're in six/eight and if this keeps on going
we'll soon be rocking in three-quarter time –
thank God the blinds are down; we're slowing . . .
relief! The postilion's horn is blowing,
the tired horses are straining for the climb.

My score is in my lap. A field of grain
would poison thought, a tree corrupt a metre –
if something's good, then serve it up again,
save paper, let the future take the strain –
manuscripts are neat, but minds are neater.

Music has bridges, proper network roads,
waterways which don't need locks and levels –
it bears its own anticipatory loads,
The Nautral Order hands it down its codes –
saints appear – a bar or so, they're devils.

God rested on the seventh day – why rest?
I'm like a fish inventing where it lives.
Life outside's a sort of palimpsest
of good and bad things nurtured at the breast –
needy, you become the need that gives.

And so I keep the blinds drawn, lock away
the milk and honey of a proffered Canaan
to travel to the concertland of play,
and in the coach, by half-light, night or day,
create the only world I can be sane in.

Stravinsky in Hollywood

You couldn't call it exile – after all
Just down the road we have a Venice,
A resting place to keep Diaghilev warm,
And all the Session Men are bronzed from tennis:
Europe's a library away, a pall
Of something chemical hangs over us.
I told them, 'Sunless as a mushroom farm.'

'Shall we listen to my Mass before
We get drunk?' Home we know is in the head,
And up the road somewhere the Schönberg train
Is crossing points into the Classic Shed –
Not the Neo-Classic! A Priceless Law!
God is good: work tells us what is God.
In California Abel murders Cain.

Shorty Rogers on the flugelhorn,
I can make something great from that.
Divide my years by Mozart's – goes three times
Almost. Everyone here's some sort of Expat,
Just like Adam. I dreamt that money was a lawn,
I mowed it, stuffed it in my agent's hat.
The studios are filming Europe's crimes.

You praise God with some skill if you have any,
But all sounds must be heard and not just written.
No paper music, no new Adorno rules,

No Kleenex tears, like Mr Britten's –
Here's Herman, Woody; Goodman, Benny,
Indexed with Huxley's *Doors* and Walter's baton,
A change of steersman on *The Ship of Fools*.

I put the carnal bells of marriage in
My compositions once and now they sound
The tocsin of my end – perhaps not yet!
Since memory may grow on any ground,
To eat the past is spirit's discipline
And Ariel's new words must be designed
Among the broken letters of the alphabet.

Scordatura

A Few Musical Re-Tunings

Looking through the catalogue of works by Liszt
provokes the thought, he can't have spent
   the whole of his life fucking.

—

Spain, land of Bullfighting and lacerating drought,
must have helped Scarlatti mould his style. Take Kk208,
   the sonata where he skins the keyboard.

—

'Musical Permafrost' says Jonathan Keates
of old Spontini. Yes, and in the deep freeze
   Gurrelieder's past its use-by date.

—

Some say, in his last quartets, Shostakovich
is composing death. Not quite the case. Rather, he's
   writing music for the dead to hear.

—

What fell on Alkan wasn't only his library
but the need of specialists to find an overlooked
   and spurious genius.

'Lassù in cielo' – not just a Verdi heroine
going home, but the suppressed transcendence
    of her creator's ruthless doubt.

'Lucifer's greatest work of art.' Why did Stockhausen
apologize? 'Man-made' catching up with 'God-made'
    deserves proper acknowledgement.

When Schönberg orchestrated Brahms's G Minor
Piano Quartet, he paid a debt to the composer
    who gave him all his rhythms.

Some artists are too great to be other than
names attached to compositions. Thus B Flat, A,
    C, B Natural, spells Everyman.

Perfectionism kept Webern's output small.
Odd that so perfect a composer as Haydn should be
    both innovative and prolific.

Inherited syphilis ruined Beethoven's hearing.
Tertiary syphilis did the same for Smetana's. In Heaven
   there'll be music but perhaps no sex.

—

Mr Kerman becomes upset if anyone reminds him
of his 'shabby little shocker'. Philippics and atonements
   seem equally de haut en bas.

—

'Polka-dotted with Chianti stains': artist
collaborators would do well to beware the comments
   of genius's amanuenses.

—

Scholarship finds it ridiculous to claim that
Schubert was the most gifted composer ever,
   but ears and heart attest it.

—

Listening to *Chronochromie*, Stravinsky jested
of M. Messiaen's 'force-de-frappe'. So many birds
   sucked in to the engines of a Jet.

Vivaldi didn't write the one concerto countless times.
He was too worldly. But Palestrina's sublimity makes it hard
　　to tell one Mass from another.

Had André Gide been a musician, would he,
when asked to name the greatest French composer,
　　have replied, 'Berlioz, hélas'?

At any one time there are only a few geniuses
composing, and mediocrities galore. Saddest are those
　　who plead, 'J'avais du talent.'

Having looked into the abyss, true originals
make their Swan Songs ordinary and cheerful –
　　not *Der Doppelgänger*, but *Die Taubenpost*.

Setting French has drawbacks and advantages:
the language's awful nasal whine; the stressless
　　syllabics of its metres.

Setting German, you are either in the forest
or the Nursery, with Goethe looking over your shoulder
   and some very stretchable vowels.

—

Setting Italian, you are in a practical Arcadia
enjoying a brevità like shorthand. The price to be paid?
   You never escape from euphony.

—

Setting English, you will always be upstaged
by your sister-art, Literature. In compensation
   you can howl and bark and vacillate.

—

Et expecto resurrectionem mortuorum? Get through
this bit before you let loose the full trumpeting
   of *et vitam venturi seculi!*

—

Whatever Musicologists say, observing repeat signs
is god-like economy. As children, we could never
   have too much of a good thing.

Fifty Years On

Every invention has something arbitrary.
GOETHE

To Carthage then I came, but this was London,
waiting for the train from rain-veiled Tilbury.
Just as I thought, I said, coming on deck
and going below. Hell is a city just

like London, but I knew I had to find
a working Hell, I'd lived too long in books.
The thing I didn't know was that I sought
A London which was in me from the start.

Not fair to this fair city. But if hearts
can bring their darkness with them, then I brought
my dark provincial hours, veranda-lit,
to match the Mayhew shadows of these streets.

I came, I saw, I conjured. I am here.
Of my ignoble comrades, most are dead.
The end is what the end is: open sea,
if mind can cross the sandbar of its fears.

Fifty years ago I'd never have
quoted a word of Goethe's. I gave up hope
to follow a more formal entropy.
Unchanging stars parade their hemispheres.

My Father Was a Businessman

So he knew my uncles were puffed with bombast
Or smoothed all over like performing seals.
They were small-time, but what they had amassed
Were big-time spoils of business deals.

My gardener Father suppressed barbaric slugs
And staked out nets to thwart the sparrows' trekking.
Beyond his lawns and wide-spread tennis rugs
Our placid country's order was for pecking.

'Old Jim's a white man,' he'd asseverate
Of some empurpled bully of the Queensland Club.
The quietness of the day precluded hate,
All plants beyond the gate encroached as scrub.

For breakfast he would eat a steaming bowl
Of 'first-break-of-the-wheat'; his luncheon plate
Was banana crushed in milk – till very old
He dined at the Commercial Travellers at eight.

His was the worst of democratic choices,
To believe in what cared not at all for him –
A Capitalist Crusoe haunted by lost voices,
A Rag Trade Prospero beyond restoring.

I conjure him, resigned and orthodox,
A slave to duty, wanting no reward.
Donald Rumsfeld's face is on the box,
Business appointing Murder to the Board.

Afterburner

For John Tranter

I knew I wasn't saying anything like exactly
what I meant, but I knew as well that it was what
I had to say. All art, I proceeded with, springs
from exaggeration, and this is due to linear time's
sheer wastefulness as a tool of understanding.

I went to the theatre, despite being warned by those
who know its dangers, and heard such 'mighty lines'
as would never be allowed in Court. Truth
to life, the programme claimed, is not the only end,
the rules insist that lives be syntax-swathed.

My neighbour had upset a tense soliloquy by opening
a box of chocolates and I noticed two young men
touching each other in the row in front. I lost the words
but gained instead a quizzical smell of almonds
and the envious quiver of remembered sex.

Yet this was strange: after some hundred hours of theatre-
going, thousands of days equipped with books and discs,
I was being tipped backwards into the sawdust memories
of down-the-road, trying to set a sort of Scrapbook up –
my childhood, such a provincial world to be born into.

Still, I knew my real concern was 'What is fuel
for understanding?' Wordsworth had to be born somewhere
and so did Wittgenstein. Back to exaggeration –
the after-shave sophistication of an uncle
was Murdoch, Mozart and Malvolio, depending.

It was then I set out on a trek for metaphor –
the missing M was money, but alas I wasn't good
at that – I got it mixed with envy, itself of course
a perfectly proper subject for research – I'd taken
eleven shillings back to school as pocket money.

A temporary assurance and dismallest companion.
Hope was running out and in a Time of Tangents
I couldn't go full-frontal. I'd open the box and so
release some old retired irrelevances, especially
The Thirty-Nine Articles of Flower Arranging.

I'd been raised an Anglican. 'In the Name of the Larder,
the Bun and the Mouldy Toast.' 'We have left undone
those things which we ought to have done.' The choir entered
with Brasso'd Cross, and the Greek Girl's breasts were
antiphoning in her sweater. I knew I loved music more than people.

The trouble was I was ten and forty and seventy and . . .
what was I? Seriously devoid of tenses for a start.
Where Jacobean poets used to fill their poems
with the very latest scientific instances, I reached
for a handbook and straightway witnessed 'Afterburn'.

So this was the glow at the tail end of my life,
this was the exaggeration I'd served so long,
the boosters were behind and what burned now
was all the fuel of living left – ahead
the prelinguistic purlieus of the gods.

Drinking Gavi with Gavin

So where in Great Nowhere might we now meet,
In what pleasant restaurant, in which offbeat street?
Such *conversazione*, such temperate munching,
Homage to three decades' improvised lunching.

Not wine connoisseurs, but going for quantity,
Ever desirous of a good white from Italy,
One unspiked by anti-freeze, a wittty *Lugana*
Or *Gavi*, its *corpore* assuring *mens sana*.

The puns and the joking, the gossip, severity –
A shy, fruitful friendship to end a dour century –
Sincere admiration, yes, probably – certainly
On my part a love of your lewd virtuosity.

Your quiet erudition – *Comm*odus! *Comm*odus!
In Cambridge it's not done to run for a bus.
What a gentleman knows, he mostly won't say,
The pain of existence, suffice to the day.

Distrustful of commerce, and most poets too,
On *Das Narrenschiff* with Auden's trim crew –
Our years copywriting to make us close kin,
Light Verse, the right verse to clothe the truth in.

My favourite dedication, 'Der Grosse Freund'.
You quoted what Freud wrote to Jung. And though joined
At the waist, like those Masters, we didn't
Have serial quarrels we had to keep hidden.

I've looked out a bottle, but only one glass.
You've gone and I go, what need of Alas?
Chiuso, the sign in the window. Dear Friend,
There's one place still open, it's at the World's End.

Goodbye to All Cats

For Roger and Patricia

After the Collectivisation of Scraps
a return to Capitalism,
investing in a well-teased mouse.

The clarinet is a cat,
the flute is a rat,
and they are chasing each other.

Smart's cat was a smart cat.
I have never had a cat so clever.
But Claudius is a better name than Jeoffrey.

Wendy Cope says writing about cats
is as bad as not being able to drive.
She has observed her poets well.

This is the Syntax Cat,
it likes its sunlight and its praise
as perfectly served up as its dinner.

As our last cat died, its urine on the table
the colour of Prussic Acid, I resolved
to rely on Plants for Lifestyle hues.

Not long after this I was knocked off
a mountain by a friendly dog.
Allies as unlikely as France and England.

Cantabile Cat, do re, miaow –
quavering its claws,
grace notes pawing at a melody.

What a beautiful Pussy you are, you are.
You won't mind being banished with Lear
to the remotest, most crepuscular star.

Philosopher Cat, doing without words,
washing Prolegomena out,
fur-balling apophthegms.

The Cat of Simple Statements.
Here. Yes. You. Me. Them.
What? Speak to my agent.

Cats as Movie Stars.
Said they'd started out as Supermodels
but had always wanted to act.

That Cat Auden put on a millstone,
is it also the horrified witness
in Lotto's Loreto Annunciation?

Both the Country Cat and the City Cat
indulge in normal shudders
when they meet the Vegetarian Cat.

The more terrible dream recurs.
It is about Death and is wholly stupid.
No place in it for any sort of cat.

Parousia with Pussy! When the end comes
among the crotons in their row of pots
she is under the house and safe again.

Farewell, my darlings! Godwin, Messalina,
Agrippina, Nero, Claudius and Flora,
Zack and Pip and Mocha. Faded into light.

Seminar Scratchcards

Closing a loophole makes a noose.

Being clouds, they hid themselves in cloud.

This philosopher's mind can't get down to Dinner Party level.

Self-effacing, but his image on a stamp.

They have given us a holiday from smiling.

Everything in this lavatory is the property of the Company.

Each pimple has an ethical dimension.

Hard Laws make Good Cases.

You have three hours left on your Credulity Card.

Bad Enough is more immediate than Much Worse.

All luck is bad.

They lived in an age which had relegated fine writing to menus.

The two sides of your brain need a Speaker to keep order.

History needed to pass through an Era of Accidents.

I have quarrelled with my name all my life.

Patriotism is the last refuge of a scoundrel and the first
resort of a government of scoundrels.

Scripture stays fresh in the Calvinator.

Christ rejoined his body on the Cross.

Christ, Jeremy Bentham and Schönberg had disciples: Mozart had
an audience.

The 'Cadaver Synod' was a disgrace, but it was funnier than 'The
Council of Trent'.

Imagine if, at The Last Judgment, we were assessed according to
our dreams and not our actions.

Christ's atonement was strangely withheld from time and
animals.

Their crematoria looked like churches and their churches like
    crematoria.
After the Reformation, there were just seven to a dozen. During the
    Counter Reformation, there were fifty to a score.
Hamlet's 'little patch of ground' held a continent's dead.
Mephistopheles thought the tempting of Faust a waste of time: he
    was looking forward to the Conference at Wannsee.
Poe's story is really about America – how the inmates took over
    the Asylum.
The barbarians waited so long they were reclassified as civilized.
Old Europe, the place which produced the old problems, but
    which, at least, is not guilty of the new solutions.
When Amphion played, stones rose up and built the city of Thebes.
Whose music is this, destroying our edifices?
Poetry makes nothing happen – would that this were true of
    Religion.
No, Auden, Yeats was sillier than us.
Successful immigrants think original inhabitants unpatriotic.
How else would they have profited in their new country?
Making love to their models saves artists time and money.
Dosso Dossi stole Titian's colours which hadn't been invented yet.
Thought starts in the middle and spreads to the extremes.
The last Stalinist regime suffocated under the weight of its
    historians.
Superior Insight – how to stay on the Left for ever.